Kay and Jay

Written and Illustrated
by Shelley Davidow

Jalmar Press

ISBN: 978-1-931061-49-0

Jalmar Press
P.O. Box 370
Fawnshin ,CA 92333
(800) 429-1192
F: (909) 866-2961
www.jalmarpress.com

About the Author and Illustrator: Shelley Davidow is originally from South Africa. Her young adult book, *In the Shadow of Inyangani*, was nominated for the first African Writer's Prize by Macmillan/Picador and BBC World. The author of numerous books, Shelley lives in Florida (USA), where she is a class teacher at the Sarasota Waldorf School.

About the Readers: These early readers are phonetically based and contain stories that young children will find enjoyable and entertaining. Each story has a beginning, middle and an ending. The stories are gently humorous while honoring nature, animals and the environment.

The six books use simple words that the early reader will easily grasp. They have been carefully chosen by a reading specialist to help students advance from the short vowels, to the silent "e", to the vowel combinations. At the back of this book is a list of sight words that should be reviewed with the child before reading the book.

About our Reading Specialist: Mary Spotts has been a remedial reading teacher for over ten years, taking countless classes and seminars to keep current in the field she loves. Her deep understanding that struggling readers need good stories — particularly if the books are phonetically based — has been an inspiration in the creation of these books. Mary has been a constant guide, ensuring that the books address specific phonetic principles while retaining a gently humorous story line.

Mary's desire to have available meaningful children's stories with decodable words and Shelley's creative talents and love of literature have been the incentive and encouragement to bring these books to production.

For Sarina

Kay was a snail. Kay slid up a rail and
sat in the sun with her tail in the air.
Jay was a snail. Jay slid up the rail to play
with Kay in the air and the sun.
Kay and Jay made snail trails on
the rail in the sun.

Kay and Jay

The sun was hot, but then the sky went gray.
Rain came. Lots and lots of rain came.
Jay slid off the rail. "Wait," said Kay.
"Wait for me!" Jay did wait.
Then Kay and Jay went to play in the rain.

Kay and Jay

Snails like rain.

Kay and Jay had fun in the rain.

Then it began to hail.

The bits of hail were big and cold.

"Help," said Kay. "I do not like hail.
Hail is not for me. I am a frail snail!"

"Hail is not for snails. Hide," said Jay.
He went to hide in a pile of mail.

Kay went to hide in a big pail.
Lots of hail came.
The big bits of hail fell on
the mail and on the pail.

Kay and Jay hid from the hail.
They had to stay under the
mail and in the pail.
They had to wait and wait.
Then the hail came to an end. Rain fell.
The rain was not so cold.

The air was fresh.
The gray sky and the rain
went away, and the sun was hot.
Jay left his spot in the mail.
Kay left her spot in the pail.
The snails slid on the hail.

Kay and Jay

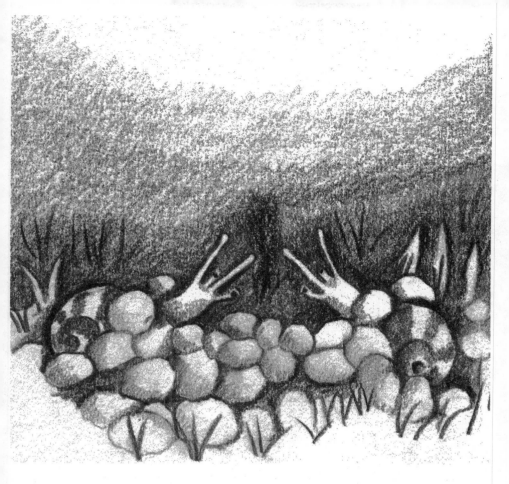

"Frail snails like hail," said Kay.

"Yes, frail snails do like hail a lot," said Jay.

The snails went to play in the hail.

The hail was very cold and wet.

The sun was hot, and the snails sat on the hail.
In time, there was no more hail.

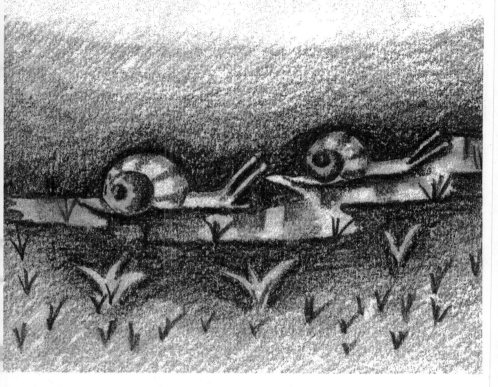

"No hail!" said Jay.

"The hail has left wet trails in the sand."

Kay and Jay went on the wet hail trails.
They came to the rail.

"The rail is wet," said Kay.

"We can slide fast on the wet rail."

So they did. Kay and Jay slid up the wet rail.
Then the snails slid fast down the
wet rail with tails in the air.

Short Vowel Sounds

a	e	i	o
fast	fell	bits	lots
	help		spot
	end		
	fresh		

Silent "e"	ai	ay	Sight Words
hide	air	Kay	began
slide	tail	Jay	cold
pile	mail	stay	under
	pail	play	down
	hail	gray	there
	rail		more
	frail		sky
	trails		away
	snails		very
	rain		
	wait		

CPSIA information can be obtained
at www.ICGtesting.com
Printed in the USA
LVHW092146141118
597188LV00001B/17/P

9 781931 061490